ACKNOWLEDGEMENTS

Publishing Director	Piers Pickard
Commissioning Editor	Catharine Robertson
Assistant Editor	Christina Webb
Illustrators	Andy Mansfield
	Sebastien Iwohn
Designer	Andy Mansfield
Print production	Larissa Frost,
	Nigel Longuet
With thanks to	Phillip Tang,
	Megan Eaves

Published in March 2018 by Lonely Planet Global Ltd
CRN: 554153
ISBN: 978 1 78701 272 1
www.lonelyplanetkids.com
© Lonely Planet 2018
Printed in China

10 9 8 7 6 5 4 3 2

Lonely Planet Offices

AUSTRALIA
The Malt Store, Level 3, 551 Swanston St,
Carlton, Victoria 3053
T: 03 8379 8000

IRELAND
Digital Depot, Roe Lane (off Thomas St), Digital Hub,
Dublin 8, D08 TCV4, Ireland

USA
124 Linden St, Oakland, CA 94607
T: 510 250 6400

UK
240 Blackfriars Rd, London SE1 8NW
T: 020 3771 5100

STAY IN TOUCH lonelyplanet.com/contact

first words
MANDARIN

Illustrated by
Andy Mansfield & Sebastien Iwohn

hello
你好
nǐ hǎo
(nee-hao)

ice cream

冰淇淋

bīngqílín

(bing-tchee-lin)

water

水

shuǐ

(shway)

supermarket

超市

chāoshì

(chao-shue)

shopping cart
购物车
gòuwù chē
(goh-oo-chuh)

cat

猫

māo

(mao)

bus

公共汽车

gōnggòng qìchē
(gong-gong chee-chuh)

dress

连衣裙

liányīqún

(leean-ee-tchewin)

dog

狗

gǒu

(go-oh)

banana

香蕉

xiāngjiāo

(sheung-jeeao)

duck

鸭

yā

(yah)

taxi

出租车

chūzū chē

(choo-zoo-chuh)

t-shirt

T恤

T xù

(tee-shoo)

fish
鱼
yú
(yue)

airplane
飞机
fēijī
(fay-jee)

chopsticks
筷子
kuàizi
(kwai-dze)

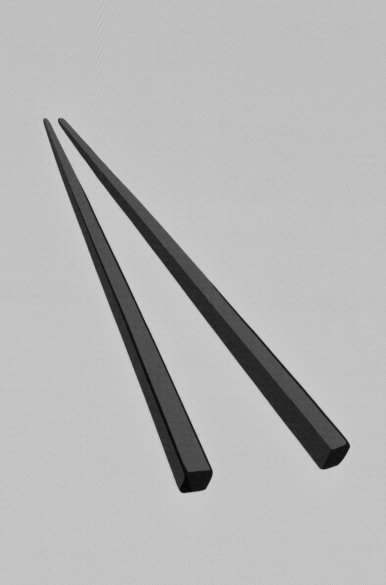

noodles

面

miàn

(meean)

swimming pool

游泳池

yóuyǒngchí
(yo-yong-chue)

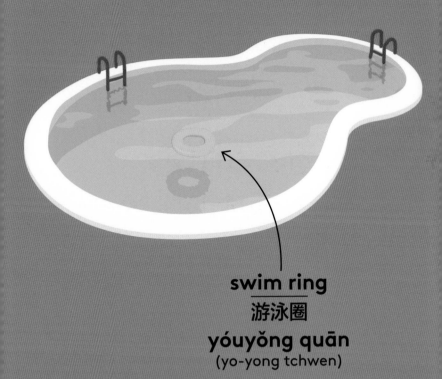

swim ring
游泳圈
yóuyǒng quān
(yo-yong tchwen)

cheese

奶酪

nǎilào

(nai-lao)

bowl

碗

wǎn

(wahn)

doctor

医生

yīshēng

(ee-shung)

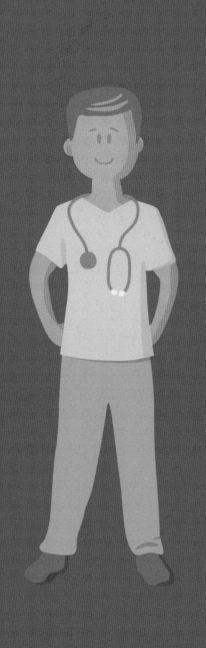

apple
苹果

píngguǒ
(ping-gwohr)

worm
虫
chóng
(chong)

beach

海滩

hǎitān

(hai-tan)

bicycle

自行车

zìxíngchē

(tze-shing-chuh)

airport

飞机场

fēijī chǎng

(fay-jee-chahng)

juice

汁

zhī

(jue)

market

市场

shìchǎng

(shue-chahng)

shoes

鞋子

xiézi

(shee-eh-dze)

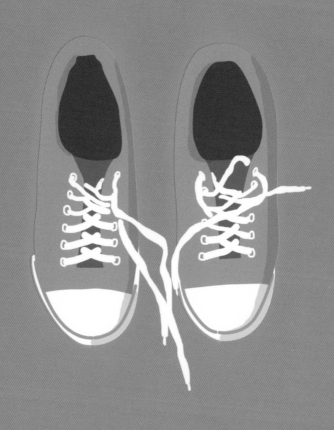

phone
***
电话

diànhuà

(dee-en-hwah)

post office

邮政局

yóuzhèngjú

(yo-jung-jue)

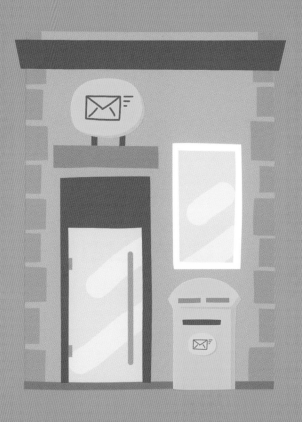

restaurant

饭馆

fànguǎn

(fan-gwahn)

hotel

酒店

jiǔdiàn

(jeeoh-dee-en)

milk
牛奶
niúnǎi
(new-nai)

chocolate

巧克力

qiǎokèlì

(tchao-kuh-lee)

car
汽车
qìchē
(chee-chuh)

hat

帽子
màozi
(mao-dze)

sunglasses

墨镜

mòjìng

(mo-jing)

chicken

鸡

jī

(jee)

train

火车

huǒchē

(hwo-chuh)

station
站
zhàn
(jan)

clock
时钟
shízhōng
(shue-jong)

toilet

厕所

cèsuǒ

(tsuh-swaw)

bed

床

chuáng

(chwahng)

house
房子

fángzi
(fahng-dze)

chimney

烟囱

yāncōng

(yan-tsong)

pants

裷子

kùzi

(koo-dze)

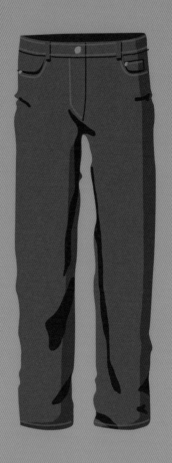

suitcase

行李

xínglǐ

(sheung-lee)

plate
盘子

pánzi
(pan-dze)

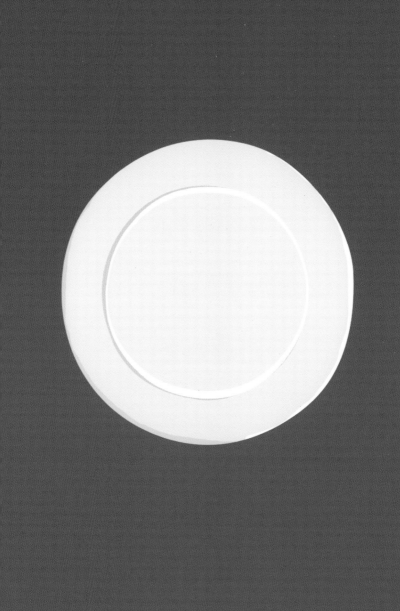

knife

刀子

dāozi

(dao-dze)

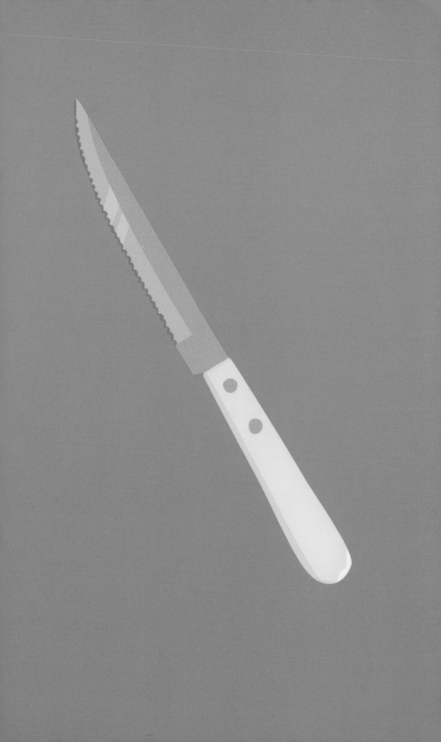

fork

叉子

chāzi

(chah-dze)

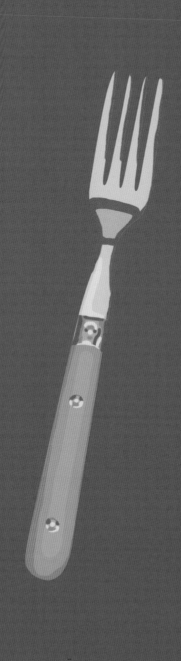

spoon
勺子
sháozi
(shao-dze)

computer
***
电脑

diànnǎo

(dee-en-nao)

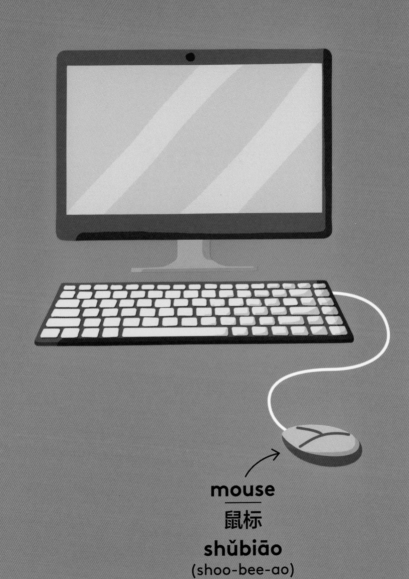

mouse
鼠标
shǔbiāo
(shoo-bee-ao)

book
书
shū
(shoo)

sandwich

三明治

sānmíngzhì

(san-ming-jue)

yes
是
shì
(shuh)

no

不

bù

(boo)

movie theater

电影院

diànyǐngyuàn

(dee-en-yeung-yoo-en)

电影院

park
公园
gōngyuán
(gong-yoo-en)

menu
—
菜单
càidān
(tsai-dan)

passport

护照

hùzhào

(hoo-jao)

police officer
___
警察

jǐngchá
(jeung-chah)

key

钥匙

yàoshi

(yao-shuh)

ticket

票

piào

(pee-ao)

sushi

寿司

shòusī

(shoh-suh)

rain

雨

yǔ

(ooe)

snow

雪

xuě

(shoo-eh)

sun

太阳

tàiyáng

(tai-yahng)

tree

树

shù

(shoo)

flower
花

huā
(hwah)

cake

蛋糕

dàngāo

(dan-gao)

cherry

樱桃

yīngtáo

(ying-tao)

ball

球

qiú

(chee-oh)

bird

鸟

niǎo

(nee-ao)

egg
蛋
dàn
(dan)

umbrella

雨伞

yǔsǎn

(yue-sahn)

panda

熊猫

xióngmāo

(shee-ong-mao)

money

钱

qián

(chee-en)

bank

银行

yínháng

(yin-hahng)

mouse

———

老鼠

lǎoshǔ

(lao-shoo)

scarf

围巾

wéijīn

(way-jeen)

gloves

手套

shǒutào

(shoh-tao)

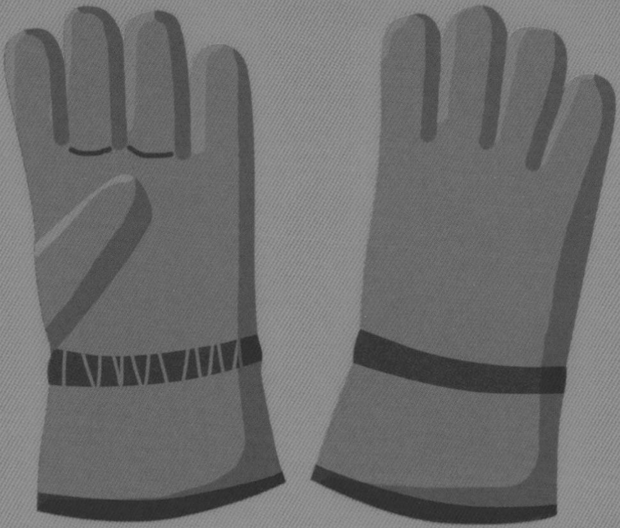

coat

外套

wàitào

(wai-tao)

hospital

医院

yīyuàn

(ee-yoo-en)

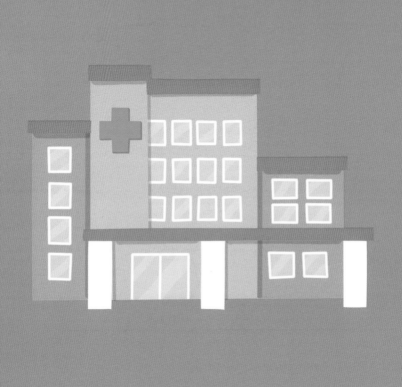

chair

椅子

yǐzi

(ee-dze)

table
桌子
zhuōzi
(jwoh-dze)

toothbrush

牙刷

yáshuā

(ya-shwah)

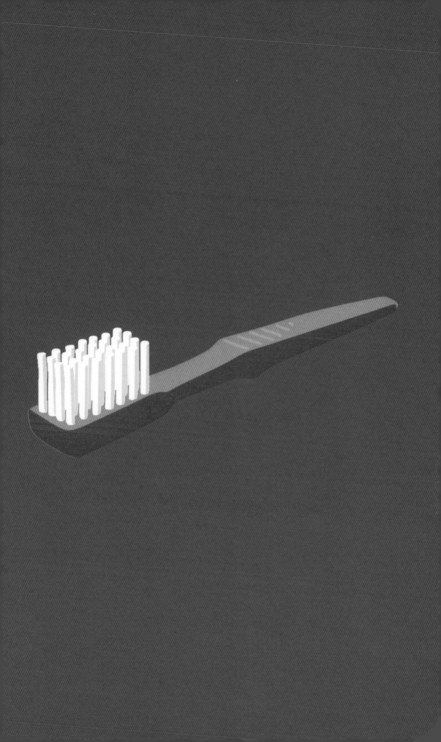

toothpaste

牙膏

yágāo

(ya-gao)

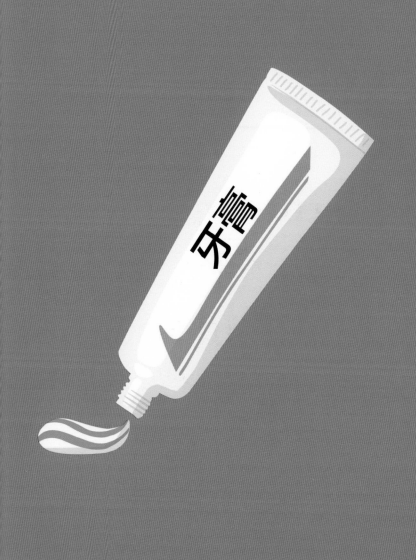

sunscreen

防晒霜

fángshài shuāng

(fahng-shai shwang)

lion

狮

shī

(shue)

mountain

山

shān

(shan)

monkey

猴

hóu

(hoh)

spider

蜘蛛

zhīzhū

(jue-joo)

rice

饭

fàn

(fahn)

pen

笔

bǐ

(bee)

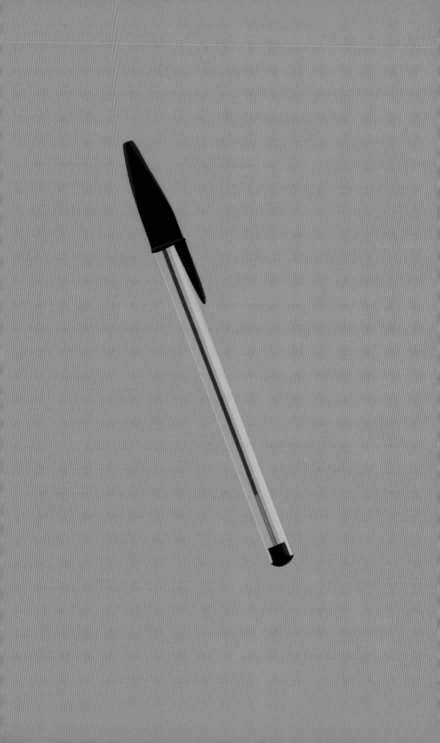

door

门

mén

(mun)

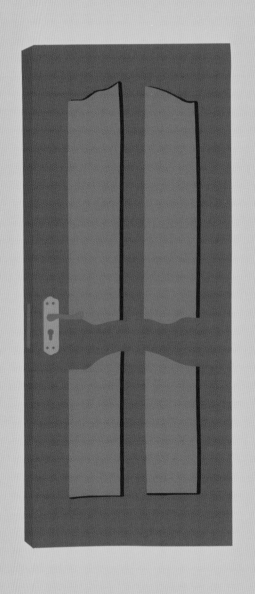

window

窗

chuāng

(chwahng)

curtain

窗帘
chuānglián
(chwahng-lee-en)

tent

帐篷

zhàngpéng

(jahng-pung)

map
地图
dìtú
(dee-too)

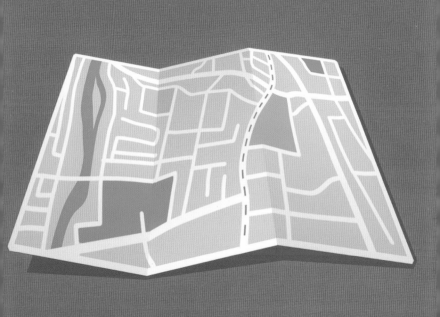

tomato
——
番茄

fānqié

(fahn-chee-eh)

moon

月

yuè

(yoo-eh)

stars

星星

xīngxīng

(shing-shing)

postcard

明信片

míngxìnpiàn

(ming-shin-pee-en)

stamp

邮票

yóupiào

(yoh-pee-ao)

boat

船

chuán

(chwahn)

goodbye

再见
zàijiàn
(dzai-jee-en)